D1297378

SandCastle 1

Capital Letters

Places

Pam Scheunemann

Publishing Company

Published by SandCastle™, an imprint of ABDO Publishing Company, 4940 Viking Drive, Edina, Minnesota 55435.

Printed in the United States.

Cover and interior photo credits: Corbis Images, Corel, PhotoDisc

Library of Congress Cataloging-in-Publication Data

Scheunemann, Pam, 1955-
    Places / Pam Scheunemann.
      p. cm. -- (Capital letters)
    Includes index.
    ISBN 1-57765-609-1
    1. English language--Capitalization--Juvenile literature. 2. Names, Geographical--Juvenile literature. [1. English language--Capitalization. 2. Names, Geographical.] I. Title. II. Series.

PE1450 .S345 2001
428.1--dc21

2001022894

The SandCastle concept, content, and reading method have been reviewed and approved by a national advisory board including literacy specialists, librarians, elementary school teachers, early childhood education professionals, and parents.

Let Us Know

After reading the book, SandCastle would like you to tell us your stories about reading. What is your favorite page? Was there something hard that you needed help with? Share the ups and downs of learning to read. We want to hear from you! To get posted on the ABDO Publishing Company Web site, send us email at:

sandcastle@abdopub.com

About SandCastle™

Nonfiction books for the beginning reader

- Basic concepts of phonics are incorporated with integrated language methods of reading instruction. Most words are short, and phrases, letter sounds, and word sounds are repeated.

- Readability is determined by the number of words in each sentence, the number of characters in each word, and word lists based on curriculum frameworks.

- Full-color photography reinforces word meanings and concepts.

- "Words I Can Read" list at the end of each book teaches basic elements of grammar, helps the reader recognize the words in the text, and builds vocabulary.

- Reading levels are indicated by the number of flags on the castle.

Note: Some pages in this book contain more than five words in order to more clearly convey the concept of the book.

Look for more SandCastle books in these three reading levels:

Level 1
(one flag)

Level 2
(two flags)

Level 3
(three flags)

Grades Pre-K to K
5 or fewer words per page

Grades K to 1
5 to 10 words per page

Grades 1 to 2
10 to 15 words per page

Aa Bb Cc

Some names of places start with capital letters.

Aa Bb Cc

We visit Monument Valley.

Aa Bb Cc

Ed plays at Riley Park.

Aa Bb Cc

Kids learn at Drake School.

Aa Bb Cc

Andy fished at Blue Lake.

Aa Bb Cc

Mary reads at Wilson Library.

Aa Bb Cc

The **Space Needle** is tall.

Aa Bb Cc

Eric swims at Valley Pool.

Aa Bb Cc

What letter does Yellowstone start with?

(Capital Y)

Words I Can Read

Nouns

A noun is a person, place, or thing

kids (KIDZ) p. 11
letter (LET-ur) p. 21
letters (LET-urz) p. 5
names (NAYMSS) p. 5
places (PLAYSS-ez) p. 5

Proper Nouns

A proper noun is the name
of a person, place, or thing

Andy (AND-ee) p. 13
Blue Lake (BLOO LAKE) p. 13
Drake School (DRAYK SKOOL) p. 11
Ed (ED) p. 9
Eric (ER-ik) p. 19
Mary (MAR-ee) p. 15

Verbs

A verb is an action or being word

129866

More Places

Carlsbad Caverns

Central Park

Boston Harbor

Bronx Zoo

Grand Canyon

Golden Gate Bridge

Mount Rushmore

DAT DUE